All Scripture references taken from the KJV of the Holy Bible, unless otherwise indicated.

## Let Them Come Up to Worship

by Dr. Marlene Miles

Freshwater Press 2024

freshwaterpress9@gmail.com

ISBN: 978-1-965772-20-1

Paperback Version

Copyright 2024, Dr. Marlene Miles

All rights reserved. No part of this book may be reproduced, distributed, or transmitted by any means or in any means including photocopying, recording or other electronic or mechanical methods without prior written permission of the publisher except in the case of brief publications or critical reviews.

## Table of Contents

God is Looking for You, *Adam* ........................ 5

Spirit, Truth, & Sacrifice ................................. 16

Bad Pastors ..................................................... 25

The *Has-Been* Worship Cherub ..................... 31

Let It Be Done in Heaven ............................... 40

Captive ............................................................ 46

Pharaoh Let My People Go ............................. 55

Ten Chances ................................................... 66

Touch Not Mine .............................................. 78

Let Them Come Up and Worship .................. 81

There Is No Holy Cow ..................................... 90

Five More Plagues .......................................... 91

Unclean ........................................................... 93

Hail Fire ........................................................... 96

The Light, the Glory ........................................ 98

What If You've Lost Your Sacrifice? ............. 101

Pharoah Spoke It .......................................... 103

Before He Came Up to Worship - David ..... 108

Before They Came Up to Worship ............... 110

Before *She* Came Up to Worship ................ 113

Moving Heaven & Earth ............................... 118

| | |
|---|---|
| **Told You So** | 121 |
| *Dear Reader* | 126 |
| **Prayer books by this author** | 127 |
| Other books by this author | 130 |
| Other Series | 138 |

# Let Them Come Up & Worship

Freshwater Press, USA

# God is Looking for You, *Adam*

God is a Spirit: and they that worship him must worship him in spirit and in truth. (John 4:24)

One particular day, God came down in the cool of the day looking for Adam and Eve. He may have asked, **Adam, where art thou?** God looked for Adam because Adam, who was made to *dress* the Garden, obviously wasn't where he was supposed to be, or where he could be found, doing what he should have been doing.

Was Adam someplace slacking off?

Dressing the Garden was Adam's job. A job assigned to a man by God is his *worship*. Whatever God made you to do, is your worship. It is not *all* your worship, but it is the lion's share of it, since you would do it more than only singing and praising, which we think is worship. You would do your spiritually assigned work more than singing, unless you were made to be a singer and a praise and worship leader. Everyone isn't; the Bible, and auditory discernment--, my ears, tell me so.

Man was made to worship. Man was made to worship the Lord in all the ways that a person can worship. That means the work of your hands, the praise from your mouth, and your Christian walk that you model before others by how you live. God expects His worship. God deserves His worship.

Are you compliant? Where is God's worship? Can God *find* you right now? Can God find you where He expects you to be, and where you are supposed to be? Can God find you doing what you are supposed to be doing, right now? Where are you *Adam*, Adam 2.0, or *whoever* you are?

When you take your kids somewhere and drop them off, say at school, the mall, or at the game, don't you expect them to be there when you go back for them? God put you here on Earth. You were born into a certain family, and you live in a certain place, for specific spiritual reasons. Then if you are not where God expects to find you and can quickly locate you, *Adam 2.0*, have you wandered off somewhere?

God formed man and woman and left them in the Garden, on assignment. He came back to visit them in the cool of the day, which, to me, means daily. But this particular day they were either out of place or missing.

No, they were hiding. Saints, when the devil can get you to willingly hide from GOD, he's really pulled a fast one on you. When the devil can have *spirits* influence your actions, or transfer and insert *spirits* in you that will make you hide, even from the presence of God, he has really done a number on you. A h*iding spirit, extreme shyness, lack of confidence, guilt, fear, rebellion, a desire for and plan to sin, unrepentant and planning to do it again, disobedience, error, a spirit of condemnation,* and also *stupidity* are some of the *spirits* that would make a person hide, and even hide from the Lord's presence or *visit.*

God is your help in this world, if He comes to you and you run from Him, *who* is going to help you?

*Where are you?* I am asking for God. *Where are you?* God is looking for His worshippers.

God does the most amazing things.

*Why?*

Because He is God.

*Why?*

Because He can.

*Why?*

Because He loves us; He does these amazing things for us, for mankind.

When I consider thy heavens, the work of thy fingers, the moon and the stars, which thou hast ordained; (Psalm 8:3A)

On occasion, doesn't your spouse make a really nice meal for you so you will not only be fed, but also pleased? Your spouse is trying to impress you. Does your spouse deserve accolades for that?

Yes.

You might say that God is showing off. God is showing off His God-ness by creating Heaven and Earth. God created Light. He divided the firmament separating the powers above from the powers below. He made the waters recede to bring ground out of the sea and created vegetation for us to have and grow food on this land, to eat. He made greater and lesser lights: the sun and moon to mark the times. Then He made animals of the air and sea. Next, He created the animals of the land, and then He formed man.

Only God could do all that. We can only approach any of those marvels by doing what God did by resting on the Sabbath. God commands that, but we would have had to do all of our other six days of work in order to enter into that *rest*.

The heavens declare the glory of God; and the firmament sheweth his handywork. (Psalms 19:1)

God feeds us, clothes us, houses us, gives us everything we need for life and for godliness. He is impressive and does mighty things. God deserves praise and He deserves His worship.

God does everything in a spectacular way because He is God; He can't help Himself. When you look at nature, for example, God did that, God made all of that, and it is marvelous. Everything He does is superlative. Where is His praise? Where are His worshippers?

> When I consider your heavens,
> the work of your fingers,
> the moon and the stars,
> which you have set in place, (Psalm 8:3A)

Regarding the above verse, the songwriter goes on to say, *How Great Thou Art* in the hymn of the same title.

When you love someone, you notice all the good things about them. You notice their beauty or attractiveness and you usually comment on it. If you tell someone else, how she's so cute, or he's so handsome, that's praise. If you tell them, to their face, *"Baby you're so fine"*--, that is worship. You notice their smarts, their wit, their sense of humor and even their ability to handle things that need to be handled. You appreciate who they are and what they can do as well as what they do for you. So, there's praise and there is worship. God deserves **both**.

To think that for even a moment the one you love is coming to visit you or is looking for you, but you hide from them, is ludicrous. In the natural, if your beloved, your fiancé, your boyfriend, girlfriend or secret crush is coming up to you, are you going to hide from them? Will you run away?

Of course, not. It makes no sense.

Then why do we hide from God, hide when we think God is looking for us? Why do people refuse to go to church with all kinds of illegitimate reasons as to why they won't go? Legitimate reasons, not withstanding, but every church doesn't have a bad pastor or bad members, or only want your money.

Okay--, let's say no one is trying to get you to go to church, then why do we hide from God by not reading our Bibles or giving Him adoration, praise, and worship?

Because the devil has run a number on those folks who hide from the presence of God in any form that His presence can be made available to us. Those who resist God are either deceived, duped, or loaded with demons who won't let them. Those folks are captives. They are still walking around; they are not locked up or in prisons, but they are spiritual captives of the devil.

If you are guilty, usually from sin-guilt and you think God is coming to beat you up, you might hide. If you are deceived and have been lied to, if you have been told that God will do something to you that He really isn't going to do, then you may hide.

that is, that God was in Christ reconciling the world to Himself, not counting people's sins against them [but canceling them]. And He has committed to us the message of reconciliation [that is, restoration to favor with God]. (2 Corinthians 5:19 AMP)

God sent Jesus to Earth to reconcile man back to the Father. God is not holding sins against us if we come to Him and repent. He does this because He first loved us.

If you don't really love God, or whomever is coming to see you or whomever you should be going to see, then you will hide, be missing, or not even care if they show up to see you. If you don't care you won't take their call or return their text.

When you love someone, you either crave to be in their presence, or at least you have so much joy to be with them and spend time with them. You don't have to be doing anything in particular, such as eating, or at a concert or on holiday, but just to be in each other's presence is so satisfying. To look at them, admire them, talk to them, is good for your soul and you will usually tell them in some way or the other, how wonderful they are and how happy you are to see them and spend time with them.

You say you love God? How much time each day do you spend with Him?

We are all invited to worship God; He wants to tabernacle with man. He wants to be with us, live with us, live *in* us. Since we are invited to Come Up & Worship, then there is no reason not to go up to worship Him, and there is no reason to hide. In Egypt, the Hebrews were physically restrained from going up to worship and that was a problem because they needed to take sacrifices. Those sacrifices were tangible, real livestock and animals.

Folks, there is nothing holding us back from worship, unless you are *spiritually* restrained; and that is what I'm talking about when I say the devil has really done a number on a person who cannot spiritually pull themselves together to at least attempt to get into the presence of God through worship.

# Spirit, Truth, & Sacrifice

We now introduce a new dimension to worshipping in Spirit and Truth, and that is **bringing a sacrifice.**

Some of you may be drawing back already because how dare I talk about bringing a sacrifice--, that means money, doesn't it? Money is often used as sacrifice; else we'd be bringing livestock to church. Pharoah, whom we will talk about a great deal later in this book said the Hebrews could go up to worship, but they couldn't go far and they couldn't take a sacrifice. Pharoah was a demonized, demon-laden, unsaved, carnal, worldly king, then why would a Christian follow Pharoah's model to worship Jehovah?

Read that again, please.

No need to pull back or cringe at the thought of bringing sacrifice to God since we aren't following Pharoah's "worship" model. Pharoah worshipped idols, not the One True God, the Only Living God. The Israelites had sacrifices and offerings going up to God 24/7. Sacrifice is part of worship, that is, if you are worshipping in Spirit and in Truth. (Selah)

Praise is telling others how wonderful another person is. The sacrifice of praise is mentioned in the Bible, the praise offering is from the mouth.

By him therefore let us offer the sacrifice of praise to God continually, that is, the fruit of our lips giving thanks to his name.
But to do good and to communicate forget not: for with such sacrifices God is well pleased. (Hebrews 13:15-16)

*Communicate*, in the preceding verse speaks of a collective gift. So there is a praise offering of the lips and also of the fruit of one's hands. Folks, it is God who gives us power to get wealth, shall we not show Him appreciation?

Worship is talking directly to a person and telling them how wonderful they are to their face. When the Lord called the Hebrews to come up and worship, He stipulated that they should bring their livestock which is their sacrifice. God is saying something like, ***I want to see you in person.***

Now, I've seen my share online of preacher critics who judge and cringe every time a pastor asks for tithes, offerings, gifts, sacrifices, seeds, and whatever else they ask for. I am not called to judge all those people and what kind of money they are asking the congregations and online audiences for, how they ask, or what they will do with it. God is in charge of that. Thankfully, He hasn't called me to that.

But all those who freak out when someone asks for money, whether they are in a service and required to give, or just watching when others are asked to give, they all must consider if money is their *god*, because it is hard for a man to part with his idol *god*. **It is most difficult for a person to think they need to come up to worship, if they are already worshipping where they are— worshipping their idol, which often times is money.**

As for me, all I need to do if I am sitting under any of those pastors or that teaching is by the Holy Spirit determine if the Spirit is talking to me and if I am supposed to participate in that.

If I am supposed to pray about it, concerning myself or others, then I do. My job is not to verbally tell anyone not to give in an offering of a church that they sit in week after week, no matter how people are asking for money. Even if they are twisting Scriptures, I am not the Holy Spirit to bring them under conviction. I am not God to determine if what they are saying is from God, if they are being prophetic or not. I am not the prophet-police. Thank God.

But, what I do know is that in my Bible the Word said that God told Moses & Aaron to tell Pharaoh to let those people go on a three day journey and let them come up and worship God, **WITH SACRIFICES.**

Hiding from the one you love or the one who loves you is counterproductive and stupid. It is anti-worship, and anti-worship is anti-marriage. I mean that in the sense that if you are married or courting a potential spouse and you don't pay any attention to them, if you never compliment them or tell them they look nice or you like the food they prepare or whatever their forte is, do you think they will care to spend time with you? People want to be where they are celebrated. So does God.

Knowing that the one you care for is interested in you, will be happy to see you, and will share time, attention and conversation with you will make you want to be in their presence. If they show no interest, joy or enthusiasm in your presence or company, you can take it or leave it. Wouldn't God be like that as well. If you keep dissing God, or the Holy Spirit for that matter, after a while they will pass you by and go to where they are wanted.

If you are being treated in a casual or aloof manner, that will not foster relationship, and certainly not marriage.

Folks, our goal is to be married to the Lamb. In this life we need to be courting the Bridegroom. The Lord is the Bridegroom and we want to marry Him.

So say something nice; that is praise, that is from the fruit of your lips. Worship also requires a sacrifice, and you NEVER attempt to go into the presence of a king without an appropriate GIFT. Worship also requires a sacrifice, and you NEVER attempt to go into the presence of a king without an appropriate GIFT. If not, in the natural the person you are interested in may lose interest in you. Guys especially, if you are trying to be cool to make the lady do all the work to get you – *oh please*. You want to be chased, that is a feminine energy, snap out of that, and stop trying to put her into a masculine energy. We seek God, but He **wants** to be found, and He will welcome us immediately, and not play games.

In the act of courting, during courtship, gifts are given--, often. In some cultures, the man who is wooing a woman will not come to her house without a gift, every time he comes to her. Is he bringing something that he can well afford, or is it a sacrifice? Financially, it may not be, but he spent time and or went out of his way to stop by the florist to bring her flowers, or by the candy store to bring her chocolates. Many times, a man who is coming to dinner will bring a beverage or dessert. He brings **something**.

Even when you go to your platonic friends' houses for meals, don't you always ask, *"What should I bring?"*

How is God any different? If you are going up to worship, you are going to God's House, ASK GOD, what shall I bring? This way you are not in shock or stunned by what the pastor may say or ask for at "offering time." This way you are not coerced or cajoled into giving what you shouldn't or giving more than you should in the service. This way you won't risk giving in error, giving too much, or not being cheerful as a giver, all of which could negate the whole process.

Saints, I ask God what I should give in the offering days and days ahead of the church service. It is set, God and I have talked about it because I've prayed about it. It is settled and my spirit man is settled about it. Once I gave LESS than God told me to give, and He wouldn't let me leave that building until I made up the difference.

To worship God in Spirit and in Truth, you bring a sacrifice, and you give it cheerfully. You count it as dead and trust that God will deal with whomever is dealing with the "sacrifices" in any church. If God has told you this is a good place to give--, this is a proper altar, then give there. If not, then get out of there and find a proper church. I recommend you read my book on how to choose a church if church or giving at your church is a problem for you. (**Choose An Altar to Choose a Church** https://a.co/d/21h42Pz )

## Bad Pastors

Some pastors are self-appointed speakers and not pastors at all. Some are devil-appointed. Some so-called pastors misuse the Word of God for whatever reasons, personal gain, fame, for whatever reasons.

Why are you sitting under such a pastor or false teacher?

It costs money to run a nice church facility, especially when everyone wants to be someone and have the nicest, biggest, newest, shiniest building of all. I saw online where one pastor named the church his own name--, he didn't even pretend to use a churchy name or a Biblical word in the name of the church.

If I'm trifling myself and don't go to church on a particular Sunday, I may say that I had church at home, First Baptist Church of (the Name of my street), but I'd never name even a home church after my own name.

Anyway --. Sitting under a false teacher is a curse and it may have come about in your life for any number of reasons:

- Bad foundation. People with polluted foundations or foundation issues may often choose a false pastor, prophet, teacher, and et cetera. They can't help it.
- Ancestral and generational curses. Unrepented sins bring on iniquity. Iniquity gives curses glue to stick to. A curse may have been spoken into your bloodline that you will always go to a bad church or have a bad pastor.
- *Spirit of Error*. If a person doesn't have the Holy Spirit and along

with that discernment, they may choose poorly--, like in life. It is not just choosing a wrong church, they may choose a wrong everything. Some are really deceived and have a false Holy Spirit which is a demon, a *familiar spirit* masquerading as the Holy Spirit.
- Bewitchment. Many times, bewitchment brings on confusion and sometimes survival mode. Confused people don't make good decisions. People in survival mode get desperate and may also choose poorly.
- Devourer is Loose. If for any reason you have robbed God, the devourer may be loose in your life. (Pray, ask God. Repent.)
- Judgment from God.

*What?*

Yes, Judgment from God – you may be required to sit under a non-teacher or a false prophet for a season as punishment for sins, iniquity, and not repenting. Best to check with God first. You may be robbed in tithes and offerings by a manipulating "pastor" demanding money from you at every turn because you or members in your ancestry robbed God in tithes and offerings and the devourer is buck wild in your bloodline. Among the devourers are the emptiers, swallowers, and destroyers. It would be best to repent right away and get it right with God.

When it comes to bewitchment you may be in a so-called church where the pastor is doing the bewitching, and you are all under his or her **spell**. Folks, this doesn't have to be a church, it could be any group or organization, even a charity, or a political campaign. It could be any place where money is asked for, or pledges and vows are made. Any time your heart strings are tugged by images of a beautiful but sick child, or an adorable homeless, shivering puppy. If you are under a spell, or certain spells, then you will be susceptible every time you see such an image or hear any stories about whatever your weakness is.

*A spell?*

Yup.

That is a foundational problem if you are bewitched and easily bewitchable. *Familiar spirits* will find you and draw you to places where you can be used and used and used all the way up if you don't get the True Holy Spirit and let Him load you with keen discernment.

And, regarding that discernment, use it. Using discernment may be difficult the first time you use it because your first response may be when you use it is the one-word answer, NO. That may sound strange coming out of your face. Those who don't have or use discernment are often nice Christians who think that being a Christian is only being nice and saying *Yes* to everything. Saints, if you are already a nice person when you get saved, are you supposed to get *nicer*? And where does warfare and spiritual violence come into play in your life if you are letting yourself become Play Doh?

How nice was Jesus?

Yes, He healed all the sick that came to Him and asked. Yes, He taught and fed the Multitude, but Jesus had folks profiling Him and trying to kill Him, what kind of *nice* should He have been when He came to oppose the works of the devil?

# The *Has-Been* Worship Cherub

God created and adorned a certain Heavenly cherub to lead worship. This cherub faltered at that assignment for his own reasons. God didn't create any fault in that cherub, all faltering was by his own doing. That cherub, Lucifer, made the choice to default on his purpose and assignment for having been created.

The word of the Lord came to me: "Son of man, take up a lament concerning the king of Tyre and say to him: 'This is what the Sovereign Lord says:
" 'You were the seal of perfection,
full of wisdom and perfect in beauty.
You were in Eden,
the garden of God;
every precious stone adorned you:

> carnelian, chrysolite and emerald,
> topaz, onyx and jasper,
> lapis lazuli, turquoise and beryl.
> Your settings and mountings were made of gold;
> on the day you were created they were prepared.
> You were anointed as a guardian cherub,
> for so I ordained you.
> You were on the holy mount of God;
> you walked among the fiery stones.
> You were blameless in your ways
> from the day you were created
> till wickedness was found in you.
> (Ezekiel 28:12-15)

Lucifer was beautiful, created to lead worship in Heaven, but he reneged on his assignment. Slack Christians, that is another reason why the devil is good at pulling people out of worship or getting them to stop worship --, he's been there and done exactly that. The devil knows what to do to keep you from coming up to worship the Lord God. Don't think you're too slick to fall for his tricks.

When I was a kid, I had a cousin who was close in age, but we were nowhere near one another in *spirit* or temperament. She was a self-willed, rebellious sort and her mother, my aunt knew it. Sadly, her mother pitted us against each other by creating envy or competition in her child towards me. It did make my childhood kind of suck.

This aunt, whom I loved, would ask her child to do some small chore for her and the child would refuse. Auntie would then say, *"If you won't do it, I'll get Marlene to do it."* Innocent me would do anything for this aunt, she was sweet to me and a very good baker. So, I'd do the errand because it needed to be done, and perhaps there was the gift of Helps in me. Not to mention, there may be baked goods such as sugar cookies coming out of the oven later on.

Well, my doing a chore that my cousin would not do for her own mother would anger my peer cousin and she would stay angry with me for days, or maybe stay perpetually angry with me because after I did the chore, my aunt would also give me money. *Oh boy, I never expected that*! I also never expected my cousin to stay angry with me either, but looking back that's what happened.

In receiving these rewards from my aunt, she really rubbed it in with her kid by being sure her child saw it. Once I remember as she handed me money cutting her eyes at her kid. So uncool, but she's an adult, what am I supposed to do or say? On my cousin's face I could see her go from shock to jealousy to hatred and bitterness all in the same moment. Did she learn from this? No. Well, she learned to hate me and be jealous of me. She did not learn to obey, honor, or respect her mother.

Besides the money and an occasional cookie or a slice of pound cake, I also got animosity, and her child never learned to obey her mother by these teachable moments. She only learned to dislike me. Man, I didn't do anything to her.

Anyway, although he was created expressly for it, Lucifer wouldn't worship God and lead the worship in Heaven. He also rebelled and got kicked out of Heaven. Subsequently God created man; man was created to worship. Whomever worships God, God will glorify, He will bless, He will prosper, He will make His own. Being glorified is better than someone saying, "Well done," to you, or giving you a slice of poundcake or money. Auntie was a great baker and a terrible teacher. The strategy she used on us may have worked on her other kids, but not on her youngest who was my childhood playmate. Parents, you must learn your children and know how to teach them.

Worship is not an errand or a chore, but guess who doesn't want man to worship God? Not only would Lucifer not worship God, but it is also as though he didn't want God to have *any* worship. Seems the devil doesn't want **anyone** to worship God. Is he jealous because that was the job that he wouldn't even do, so he doesn't want anyone to take his place?

It's probably deeper than that--, far more evil than that as we may find out as we delve into this issue.

God formed us especially to the praise of His glory, so the devil wants to stop mankind from worshipping God. You've got to really think a lot of yourself if you think you can stop God. This is Jehovah Sabaoth; He has **never** lost a battle.

Unlike my peer cousin who never tried to stop me, she just didn't want to do it herself, the devil's plan is to STOP worship. Not only that, but he has also formed many ways and tactics of stopping us at our assignment to worship God.

The devil gives man false things, wrong things, substitute things to worship. Recall, God is looking for those who will worship Him in Spirit and in Truth. Diluted or polluted worship is no worship at all. It is doublemindedness and the doubleminded man will receive nothing from God.

That's like being on a date with your beloved but your head, or their head is turning at every other person who walks by. I hope you've never been on a date with someone, but you felt as though you were not with that person, or the person was not with you because they were eavesdropping on everyone else in the room or somehow involved in what others were doing instead of with you, in conversation or getting to know you.

Even down to the waiter, they seem to have a better rapport with the waiter than with what was going on at your dinner table. Yeah, that kind of non-attention and lack of focus, which boils down to lack of interest will not foster *relationship*. Will that person get anything from you later? Of course not. By the end of the evening there is nothing more but disdain, disinterest on your part and you never want to see them again. None of us are God but as God does, we will lightly esteem those who lightly esteem us. Can't help it, really.

The devil wants the worship for himself. He tempts man to worship him. No, what am I saying? The devil asks man or **tells** man to worship him. He doesn't always say, *instead of God*, but that is his intention. The devil can steal worship or trick a person into worshipping him. Yes, he is that clever. Folks, the devil is not necessarily a quick study; don't underestimate him and his tactics.

Most often he sets traps and snares and captures man like he's some kind of an animal, to physically keep him from worshipping. It doesn't even have to be physical captivity; being captured spiritually will keep a person from worshipping and that person may not ever know that they are captive or why they no longer have the drive or impetus to worship, if they ever had it. Spiritual captivity can do that to a mind while the body is still living the same life that it has always lived. If a person is not spiritual, they will **never** figure this out. They may go to the doctor for vitamin pills or shots or even medicine for depression, but this is a spiritual problem, not a physical or medical problem.

## Let It Be Done in Heaven

In Heaven, the 24 elders cast down their crowns crying, *Holy, Holy, Holy.* The angels worship. The beasts around the throne all worship 24/7.

We must agree with Heaven, *Let it be done in Heaven as it is in Earth.*

There should be 24/7 worship coming from this planet up to the Throne of God. Heaven and Earth should **agree** and that is why God is looking for worshippers. Worship is happening 24/7 in Heaven; it should also be happening 24/7 in Earth. God inhabits the praises of His people. If you are looking, finally looking for God, He needs praise to descend into your presence.

God rides on Thrones, those are the highest order of angels, let's then say the "tracks" that those Thrones ride on is praise and worship, if you aren't sending up any praise or worship, there is no way for God to get here or get to you. As in our date example, there is no interest in God getting to you if there is no worship going forth to Him.

This would be one very strong reason the devil doesn't want you to worship or praise. If you are cold toward God, then God won't be on the way to you or your situation. In this state, the devil can continue to run roughshod over you.

Just as with idols, if you don't give them worship and none of your ancestors have laid down a path or any tracks for them to get to you, they cannot get to you. In the presence of God is fulness of joy and at His Right Hand are pleasures forevermore. But you need to get into God's presence.

Not just worshippers, but those who will worship Him in Spirit and in Truth. Please note a difference here, the devil and his cohorts will take any kind of worship, even if you didn't mean to worship. They will conflate a little bit of attention for worship and *as* worship. God is particular about what He calls worship. Your attitude and adoration must be in Spirit and in Truth, not something half-way or half-hearted or accidentally crying when the rest of the congregation is singing. That's not worship.

This is why a lot of people can't get into the Presence of God even though they are singing and dancing. Not only that, a lot of "worship" songs are not worship towards God at all. Instead, too many songs are about the person singing about how *they* will go into worship or that they have come to worship. Worship of God is about God; it is not about the worshipper. Ask yourself, how many *I's* and *me's* can be in a worship song about **God**?

A song can be instructive as to how to worship, but that is not worship. Neither is a slow song worship just because it is slow. And, as said, just because you get emotional, or you feel a certain way during the singing of a song does not make that worship, either. You could feel a certain way during a slow secular song, that is not worship to God--, but warning: It could be worship. Now you must know who or what you are singing praise and worship to... yourself, some other person, some other entity, or the Lord God?

You can worship without music. You can worship in the congregation and also at home, privately as well. Man is made to worship; he most likely is worshipping something or someone 24/7. Yes, even when he is asleep.

Oh, saints of God, when we are asleep sometimes our spirit could be roaming about; do we even know? If we are absent the body, like ever, we should be present with the Lord. If we are present with the Lord, won't we be worshipping Him? If we are absent the body to worship, but we are not with the Lord, **who** has stolen us, even temporarily? Who has taken or captured us in the night, to *take* our worship?

> When I was in distress, I sought the Lord; at night I stretched out untiring hands, and I would not be comforted. (Psalm 77:2)

Pray that the Lord is always with you, even and maybe especially in the night hours. Amen.

> We are confident, I say, and willing rather to be absent from the body, and to be present with the Lord. [9] Wherefore we labour, that, whether present or absent, we may be accepted of him.(2 Corinthians 5:8-9)

It is believed that the Apostle John fell into a trance and was in Heaven seeing all that was there. John was present with the Lord, and he even wrote about it to tell us.

When you have a heart of worship you will always worship. When you have a heart to worship God you will always worship God. If even for one moment you are absent from your body, in a trance, in sleep, even in death, your spirit should make a beeline to God.

The Words of the Lord are still resounding: ***Let My people go and let them come up and worship.***

Saints we are invited, we are welcomed. We are expected. We are commanded, actually. If we can't get to God, we make it opportune for Him to get to us and when He gets to us, whatever condition we are in that is not Godly, He will bring us out of it.

# Captive

By the rivers of Babylon, there we sat down, yea, we wept, when we remembered Zion.
We hanged our harps upon the willows in the midst thereof.
For there they that carried us away captive required of us a song; and they that wasted us required of us mirth, saying, Sing us one of the songs of Zion. How shall we sing the Lord's song in a strange land? (Psalm 147:1-4)

There we hung our harps; how can we sing the song of the Lord in a strange land? Israel was captive in Babylon, and they required a song of them.

*They*? Who is *they*? People who want you to entertain them? Are the captors mocking God by asking for a *song, like a slave owner asking a slave to sing a spiritual*? Whatever worship song you have to the Lord is to the Lord, it is not for entertainment of the oppressor. Well, it could be for irritation of the oppressor. It could be to soften the heart of the oppressor and perhaps proselytize him and win him to Christ. Okay, we will sing for that reason, but not to entertain the jailer.

But before Babylon the Hebrews were captive in Egypt for 430 years. Not only were they captive, but Egypt was a land of many idols, false *gods, goddesses*, interferences, distractions, and false worship.

An idolatrous person is easily distracted by idols. It's like the kid who goes into the toy store and wants **everything** he sees. Parents, you've got a job on your hands. You need to break that *spirit* off your kid. If he took it honestly from one or both of you, then either or both of you need prayers and deliverance. That *spirit* will not just go away on its own, it will only get stronger, and what your child will want and covet, and worship will only get bigger, more expensive, and more dangerous as he grows up.

Deal with deliverance early – it is best. If you are the parent, do it for your child. Don't leave it for the child; he may never do it.

Whether child or adult, the person who is gluttonous is an idolater. All these *spirits* are part of *whoredoms*. People under that strongman are easily tempted, often swayed, and drawn away easily by *lust* and another *lust*, and another *lust*. That's the man who is on a date, but his head is on swivel. That person most likely falls *a-lusting,* often.

*How do I know this?*

The Bible tells us so.

But every man is tempted, when he is drawn away of his own lust, and enticed. (James 1:14)

For all that is in the world, the lust of the flesh, and the lust of the eyes, and the pride of life, is not of the Father, but is of the world.(1 John 2:16)

Lust of the eyes--, the eyes are never full.

Hell, and destruction are never full; so the eyes of man are never satisfied. (Proverbs 27:20)

When the Hebrews finally got out of Egypt, they fell *a-lusting*. And what did they lust for? Food. Cukes, melons, garlic; they missed the food of the oppressor. Seriously. Yeah, they were very cheap "dates." All they needed was a tasty meal and they'd fall down and worship.

Folks, you won't just fall *a-lusting* unless there is idolatry, which is a subsidiary of *whoredoms* in you.

You want, want, *want*—everything you see and even some things you don't see, but things you only imagine.

> The Lord is my shepherd, I shall not want. (Psalm 23:1)

Not *wanting* means you aren't lacking anything, but it can also mean that you are **not** driven by lust, and cravings, and yearnings, and other feelings that can lead to desperation and very poor choices. If you are a coveter, you are the perfect candidate. Any kind of cheese in any kind of trap or a net can catch you.

Saints, this is why we fast. It is to learn how to resist things and how not to give into our flesh and emotions all the time. Yes, to be delivered from emotional eating and also flesh cravings. I once fasted chocolate for an entire year just to prove that I could get over it. *Why?* Because I really needed to get over it. Praise God, now I can take it or leave it, but it took an entire year.

Did the Hebrews worship any of the alleged 1500 Egyptian *gods* and *goddesses* that they were said to worship? I believe they did. After all, they were there for 430 years of slavery, and people tend to assimilate with their environment and captors, just to *get along*. Well--, **they ate the food.**

Also, we note that the Egyptians didn't start worshipping Jehovah as far as the Bible states. So who was influencing whom? The Hebrews were not spiritually strong when they were under judgment and sent into captivity; they were weak because of their sins.

Many times, initiations and worship can start with food. As we learned from their behavior in the Wilderness, they had some kind of a covenant with the food of the Egyptians.

Sodom and Gomorrah started with food, and we know how low they descended in those twin cities. Eating food dedicated to idols will initiate a man and also bring him down.

> That ye abstain from meats offered to idols, and from blood, and from things strangled, and from fornication: from which if ye keep yourselves, ye shall do well. (Acts 15:29)

How did food and fornication get in the same verse? I told you, already. They travel together, they are under the same strongman of *whoredoms,* and they both are caused by idolatry. It is often why dates that lead to fornication many times start with "dinner."

Once free from Pharoah and Egyptian slavery, some Israelites wanted to go back to Egypt, complaining about the Wilderness because obviously territorial powers were calling them back. A *territorial spirit* can't just call you back to a place unless you participated in some way while you were in that place in some form of *worship*. Else, you'd easily shake the dust and get out of Dodge and never look back.

Lot's wife looked back. Ever wonder why? She had some covenant with something or someone there. Maybe she just loved her house and was going to miss it and its lovely décor. Maybe she had "friends" there that she lunched with every week. Something was calling her back, so she turned to give another or a last look. Or, was she undecided as to whether she wanted to leave or stay? If her physical body had left Sodom and Gomorrah, but her heart was still there, then that soul tie would inhibit her future worship and successful life, and especially her marriage, forever.

I believe by looking back and then turning to salt the account is telling us that she did not want to leave those sinning cities. Lot's wife looked back, but God does not do that turning back thing.

And Jesus said unto him, No man, having put his hand to the plough, and looking back, is fit for the kingdom of God. (Luke 9:62)

By turning back, Lot's wife was no longer fit for service.

This is why in my life I do not go back. It would take the voice of God to make me go back to anything; I don't go back.

We think we don't worship idols; but do we? Whether Lot's wife wanted to go back or not, she looked back and that was enough for her to turn into a pillar of salt. Sometimes just ***looking*** at a thing is worship. Just giving it attention is a form of worship. Any of us may be very surprised how a demon, devil, or an idol *god* or *goddess* can pull worship out of us. Thinking on the horrible thoughts and ideas that they introduce into your mind, whether you carry it all the way to sin or not, is still worship.

## Pharaoh Let My People Go

God is looking for His worshippers. God is looking for His people.

In addition to tricking a man into hiding himself from God, the devil can also hide or cover a man to interfere with his worship of God.

As I was reading the account in Exodus of Pharoah and his hardened heart, it occurred to me that by asking that one question over and again, God was very clear on what He was looking for, and what His goal was.

Starting in Exodus 7, God told Moses and Aaron to go see Pharoah and say, **Let My people go that they may serve Me.**

These ten plagues were about letting the people go, but it was about letting them go with a purpose.

**Let My people go that they may serve Me**, was said at least ten different times on ten different days and occasions to Pharoah. This is the same as saying, *Let My people go that they can come up and worship Me.*

God will contend with those who contend with you. let's look at how God contended with Pharoah.

Some of the plagues affected all, some only affected the Egyptians. None of the Egyptian plagues only affected the Hebrews—so had God's people finally learned their lesson?

Only the first three Egyptian plagues affected the Hebrews. Was God also showing the Hebrews that He is greater than this *god* and this *goddess*, et cetera? In those first plagues, God was showing Pharoah and the Egyptians as well and by chance Pharoah and some of the others may put down their worship of idols and begin to worship the One True God.

Were the Hebrews, or some of them serving some of those idols?

Well, it is possible, as said, because idolatry was in them, else they would not have fallen *a-lusting* in the Wilderness And, they were still idolaters because in the Wilderness they built the idol golden calf to worship – idolatry was still in them, even after 430 years of hard labor--, slavery. We know it was still in them because **none** of them went into the Promised Land – their kids did, but they didn't make it in.

*Idolatry – whoredoms* doesn't just come out on its own, it has to be cast out, forced out, and resisted to keep it from returning.

Pharoah and the Egyptians of the Bible invite idol *gods* and *goddesses* by worship, by culture, by origin. By virtue of where they live. It comes with the territory. It was built into them; Egyptian parents might as well tell their kids, *These are the gods that you will worship.*

We can compare this to superstition; superstition is a form of idolatry. It is also witchcraft. If you believe a certain thing will help you when it won't, this will protect you, and it won't. If you believe that this will cause this, that, or the other, and it doesn't—, we call it superstition, another name for idolatry. Once you do it, that is an initiation into worshipping the *god* or *goddess* of that *thing*.

When you are trying to get what you should be getting from God from any other entity, or in any other way than from God, that is idolatry. When you are giving love, attention and anything else of value to anything or anyone that is not God; that is idolatry.

When you give and expect nothing in return, that is Love, when you expect something in return that may be love, but it is worship with a quid pro quo. That may be worship, but it is not pure, so it is not in Spirit and Truth.

If you do something because you think you are supposed to do it, or you have been made or trained to do it and there is no emotion or soul in it, that is empty service. That is lip service because you really don't mean it.

Does the woman who buys flowers every Friday to put in front of her Virgin Mary statue at her home do it because she loves Mary? Is it a habit? Does she do it out of tradition and obligation? Or, does she just like flowers there and thinks it's pretty?

How can she have a relationship with *Mary*? Mary is dead and the dead know nothing. **The Queen of Heaven has masqueraded for centuries as the Virgin Mary.** Led by the Catholic Church—, even by the Pope, and their ancient traditions, look at all the worship this demon has gotten and is still getting. That is stone cold idolatry and that lands people in piping hot hell.

God searches the heart, but the act of doing even the simplest things for an idol is worship no matter what intent is behind it. Whether a person realizes what they are doing or not, if it is idolatry, it is idolatry.

**They know not what they worship.**

Ye worship ye know not what: we know what we worship: for salvation is of the Jews. (John 4:22)

Some know what they are doing as they serve an idol for gain, while trying to circumvent or bypass God, leaving Him out of the equation. Some think like Pharoah, and many others in many cultures, even today that they can add idol upon idol, and be more protected, more powerful, and even richer. It is still idolatry. At some point that idol will want blood, so there will be disaster in their lives somewhere if they are not serving the One True God, Jehovah.

Sad thing, saints of God, the devil has no warranty. If you are dissatisfied for any reason with anything that he has promised or done for you—there is no recourse. When he is demanding a blood sacrifice, you can't very easily back out of the deal and say, *Never mind*.

There are no returns, no complaints department, and no *never minds* in Hell. Only God can get you out of the captivity of Hell, and only while you are alive. Yes, captivity is in regions of hell and torment. Captivity and demonic prisons are run by Satan and his demons and if it is not in hell, it is hell by virtue of who is running it. So you need to get out of hell, or *parts* of you need to get out of hell because you can be captured by *parts*. What do I mean? Is there a *part* of your life that is not working? Is there one organ in your body you are having an issue with? That's what I mean by *parts*.

So, you need to know if you are in hell or if any part of you or your life is **in** hell, even while you are on this side of life—while you are alive. There is no rescue from hell after death. So do not do things that will land you in hell, either now, or in eternity. Especially, don't trade your soul for *things and stuff.*

The devil doesn't really know who you are, but God does. God knows what you need, what you don't need, what you should have, and what you shouldn't have and the correct timing for all of that. The Lord does not make mistakes, so there is no need for returns or a complaint department in Heaven. Everything God does is fully correct and guaranteed, every time.

But if you've decided on the cheap knock off by worshipping idols instead of the One True God, Jehovah, because the idols promised to be faster and easier than God. That idol will have you thinking that there are no requirements (up front) and you want it by **yesterday** anyway---. BIG MISTAKE! That's idolatry, big time.

They have mouths, but they speak not: Eyes have they, but they see not: They have ears, but they hear not: Noses have they, but they smell not: They have hands, but they handle not: Feet have they, but they walk not: Neither speak they through their throat. (Psalms 115:4-8)

Having a false sense of security when there is **no** security, makes a person a sitting duck, a target--, a fool. There is no lucky rabbit's foot. There is no lucky hat, shirt--- no *lucky* anything; all that is superstition and idolatry.

Except the Lord build the house, they labour in vain that build it: except the Lord keep the city, the watchman waketh but in vain. (Psalm 127:1)

If you think you have idols watching over you and protecting you, you'd better think again.

Countries and people who delve into and are saturated in idolatry are easily conquered by enemies. The main reason is that God takes His hands of protection off those idolaters. Another reason is that they are easily tempted and distracted; so they are powerless and also unfocused. Another reason is that idols don't have the power you may think they have; God is the greatest power. Power belongs to God.

A third reason is they don't care about you; they don't **love** you; they only want your worship now and later on add to that, they want sacrifices. Imagine, there you were not wanting to bring sacrifices to the only living God, while the dead idols want blood sacrifices from humans. Everything an idol does is ultimately for them, not for you.

God causes us to dwell in safety in the land and He gives rest to His beloved because He **loves** us.

To worship in Spirit and in Truth, you need your whole soul and your whole focus. You may sincerely believe you are sincerely worshipping your idols and your intent, the spirit of your worship may be there, but they are not the One True God, therefore there is no Truth in that relationship. Further, they have not given you full disclosure of what is required to deal with them or get favors from them.

**They are subprime *gods* to the max.**

They don't have a Heaven to put you in, but their every direction puts you on the path to hell. No one who loves you would set you on the road to purgatory and hell.

God first LOVED us. We need LOVE to worship in Spirit and in Truth, else it is false worship. You can't fake worship, although some try. The Kingdom of Heaven works by Love, even the Gifts of the Spirit work by LOVE.

God is Love. Only God is love. These devils, demons, and idols *gods* have no Love, if they did why would they have fallen from Heaven, and forcefully at that?

## Ten Chances

We won't go into the reasons why Pharoah resisted God for ten plagues. That is clearly stated in the Bible, and expounded upon in my book, **Lord, Let the Devil Overplay His Hand**. But I will say that it seems that Pharoah not only thought he had all the *gods*, but he also thought he had the best *gods*. So many *gods* that anyone would get tired of having so many "powerful" and important idol *gods*—the most important idol *gods*.

Even with all those *gods*, not one of them could defeat the One True God.

"Who is this God of the Hebrews that I should let you go?" Pharoah, who was probably Ramses II, wanted to know.

Well, Mr. Pharoah was about to find out.

Biblically, ten represents the fullness of quantity. Getting ten chances to correct any mistake is a great Mercy. It is Grace. Most parents will only count to three and if you don't do what they say, you're gonna get it, or you may lose something or some privilege that you dearly want. In a hostage situation, how many counts or chances will the perps get before a SWAT team descends on them? Probably not ten.

Three strikes you're out of the whole ballgame. Three strikes will lock a person up for a long, long time.

But Pharaoh got **ten** counts.

Was Pharoah wise enough to know he was getting **ten** chances or was he foolish enough to think that the first nine plagues were victories because his little pocket idol *gods* beat the God of Israel?

*Oh pls.*

*Dear Reader,* today we are not focusing on what Pharoah did or why he did it, today we will look at the One True God, Jehovah. What did God do to, yes prove that He is surely great, but because of Love, it wasn't just about God proving His wonderfulness. We should all know that anyway.

God came at Pharoah ten different ways and that was three steps up from the seven ways the enemy should flee when they come upon the people of God. Yes, God proved that He was ten times better than anything Pharoah had defending himself and his kingdom. But did Pharoah have sense enough to flee when it was Jehovah coming against him for his stubbornness?

> He shall subdue the people under us, and the nations under our feet. 4 He shall choose our inheritance for us, the excellency of Jacob whom he loved. (Psalm 47:3-4)

> He suffered no man to do them wrong: yea, he reproved kings for their sakes;. Saying, Touch not mine anointed, and do my prophets no harm. (Psalm 105:14-16)

God's people were under unbearable bondage and hardship, they were under hard labor in Egypt. Not only that, the prophecy and the time that they should be in captivity was over and they should have been able to come out of slavery. But, Pharoah held them captive.

Are you in captivity? Well ask yourself are you? Are you free? Are you free to honor God, to praise, worship and serve the Lord? If not, perhaps you are in captivity. Do you think your own thoughts, or are you bombarded with ridiculous or evil ideas that come from who knows where? Are you oppressed? Are you distressed? Are you living an abundant or redundant life-- , the same horrible life that your oppressed parents lived? If your life is not abundant, then you may be captive.

Do bad things keep happening to you? Do you choose incorrectly way too often? Does what you want to happen rarely or never happen? Are you in pain, constant pain? Are you suffering from illnesses and diseases? Is your marriage or family at risk? You are most likely in captivity.

You are not a zoo animal, but you could have been born in captivity. If your parents were in captivity when you were born, then you were not born free. Don't believe me? Hebrews were captive in Egypt, when they had a child, was that child free or also a slave? Okay then.

Are you saved and still don't understand why life isn't as it should be? Don't blame people. People didn't cause this. The kind of captivity I'm talking about is spiritual. Now people may come into play and act out their parts in your life, but what you are living and going through is foundational and it is because of captivity, unless you are *in Christ* and **fully in Christ.**

Please don't be of the ilk of people who look way across wherever and pick out a people group or a *nation* that has nothing to do with you and that you have nothing to do with, have never met and most likely will never meet and decide that they are the reason your life sucks. Or ascribe to them a fear that your life will suck in the future because they exist, unless they are coming to attack you, and they are not.

YOUR PROBLEMS ARE SPIRITUAL. YOUR PROBLEMS ARE PERSONAL AND SPIRITUAL. THEY MAY BE ANCESTRAL AND FOUNDATIONAL, the guy down the street or across the country or on the other side of the world, none of which are threatening you, are not your problem. If you believe that foreigners are your problem that would be as the Hebrews are in slavery in Egypt and they are complaining that the Amalekites, Hittites and Gibeonites won't let them into the Promised Land.

What Promised Land? They don't know anything about a Promised Land, yet. Until you get yourself out of your bondage, out of slavery in Egypt, you are not even or ever going to MEET those other –*ites*.

Folks, until you get saved and get fully into Christ, you are in no position to hate, oppose, or fight anyone--, that means any other nation, so stop it. Don't be foolish. Further, if you get all into Christ, God will make things right for you. It doesn't mean that you won't need to fight, and especially spiritually, but the battle will be far different than what you think it is. Right now, outside of Christ, or saved and just on the fringes of the Kingdom and not truly in it, you are only waging or proposing a flesh war. In that, you will lose; without God, you will lose. Watch Pharoah and see what I mean.

When *nations* are spoken of in the Bible, those are *spiritual entities*. Yes, *spirits* can inhabit flesh bodies, but we don't fight **people** unless GOD explicitly says so.

If a *nation* is keeping you from worshipping God, then you've really got a problem. That nation should be dealt with, spiritually. That is what God was doing idol by idol via the Egyptian plagues.

Are you okay with the level of captivity you are under? Have you and the jailer gotten to be buddies, and you like being captive? (God, I hope not.) Is what is being required of you hardship, labor and impossible? Have you gotten to the place where you can't take it anymore?

Is the **time, the season, the sentence** of your captivity up?

That's complicated because if you are under judgment from God, then you must repent and repent fully, repent quickly.

So, now that you have fully repented, then the time of your captivity should be up. If God doesn't send a Moses or Moses and Aaron or some other prophet to announce that the season of your captivity is over, **then in the authority of Christ and the Word of God, <u>you</u> prophesy it yourself, over yourself.**

Are you coming out of bondage and oppression?

Know this, if the time of your captivity has ended, the Word of God says, **I will not leave your soul in hell.** The Lord will come and get you or send a deliverer.

When God comes or sends His power, His Word or His mighty Angels, alone or with a human deliverer, you won't hide, *will you*? When God stepped in the Garden that day to talk with Adam and Eve, surely, He knew where they were; He's God, He knows everything. If we make our bed in hell, God knows. God also knew that they had sinned, and He knew that they had been captured by the devil.

For your consideration, might God have come to deliver Adam and Eve, but they were hiding? I still haven't seen a Bible account of Adam or Eve repenting to God. Did they ever say that they were sorry? How can they possibly be delivered unless they at least start with repentance.

But instead, they hid.

Demons, devils and the like will make a person hide even from what is good for them, even from what is best for them, even from the Word of God, and from deliverance itself. There is no opposition for a demon-possessed man to go to a non-Word, non-deliverance, party church, but if he were to go to a deliverance ministry his family might object, he might be sick that day, his car may not start and he may have the craziest thoughts as to why he should not go to that church that day, or ever. That is the devil making him **hide** from his deliverance.

Demonic and witchcraft slavery profits the evil kingdom and those who work for it and within it. Slavery is non-profit, it is a total loss for the spiritual slave. Working is worship; working for free is slavery and it is also worship. So even if you have declared a new season and that season is freedom, will the enemy let you go?

What we learned in Exodus is that God will let even a slave go when these certain conditions are met that we have been sharing in this book, along with the newly released person who is coming up to worship the Lord God. If there is a purpose in your being set free, God will come Himself, or send someone, spiritually and or naturally to get you out of captivity. As long as you are alive, as long as there is life, there is hope. Even if you are in captivity, as long as you are alive you can get out. After death, that is another whole story which you will not like. Even if you think your idols are helping you and giving you the good life on this side, hell is another whole story, and it is eternal.

Demons (fallen angels) that Pharaoh served who posed as or were considered *gods* or deities didn't want to lose their worship. They didn't want the worship that they may have normally gotten to go to Jehovah. Plus, when a man worships God, more power is available to that man. Demons and even wise politicians know that there is strength in numbers, so they want to keep you right where you are. You can't rule over a people if you don't have any *people,* so they want to keep you right where you are.

But God says, **Let my people go, so they can come up and worship Me.** Built into that is the people will come up and worship God, but they will first turn off their worship to idols. To worship God in Spirit and Truth you must be worshipping only Him and not everything or anything or anyone else. *Whoredoms* is worshipping pretty much anything. A person saturated in *whoredoms* cannot be trusted to be faithful.

## Touch Not Mine

Ten Egyptian plagues was a fullness of plagues against Pharoah and his people. We know that each of the Egyptian plagues countered the authority and power of an Egyptian-worshipped *god* or *goddess*. But each plague did not touch God's people. Only certain ones…

For all the gods of the nations are idols: but the Lord made the heavens. (Psalm 96:5)

God did not let the last seven plagues touch the Hebrew slaves. We can suppose there was no guilt on their part in regard to the idols that were being disgraced; we can believe that Hebrews did not worship those gods. Or, Pharoah wasn't getting it and God didn't want to take His people through all that a demon possessed and false-god obsessed man would endure.

Perhaps after the third plague the Hebrews straightened up and started serving God the right way. For whatever reason, Gods ways are higher than ours, but sending Moses and Aaron to Pharoah to say, Let My People go so they can come up and worship Me is like after 400+ years, God is giving them an open book test, God is giving them the answer:

I WILL LET YOU GO IF YOU COME UP AND WORSHIP ME. God even said it ten times and with signs and wonders so His people would notice, pay attention, hear, learn, sit up, stand up, and walk right. That is Mercy, and that is Love. Can't we see that?

- 4$^{th}$ Plague: Flies. A good shepherd keeps flies away from the heads of the sheep. Jesus is THE Good Shepherd, so no flies for His own.
- 5h Plague: Livestock died. The people of God needed those cattle

and livestock to offer sacrifice to the Lord.
- 6$^{th}$ Plague: Boils.
- 7$^{th}$ Plague: Fiery Hail.
- 8$^{th}$ Plague: Locusts, so thick they blocked the sun as well as ate up everything.
- 9$^{th}$ Plague: Darkness.

Killing of firstborn children: The tenth plague. This was a plague where God tested the obedience of His people. Kill the Passover Lamb. Strike the doorposts and the lintel with the Blood of the Lamb, prepare the lamb and eat it a certain way, and get into your house and stay there.

Obedience is critical because idolaters are not obedient to God; that is the hallmark of idolatry, disobeying God and doing what you want and eventually what the demon *god* tells you to do. I know this because that's what Pharoah did and he along with his army all got drowned in the Red Sea and died.

# Let Them Come Up and Worship

Moses asked that the Hebrews be allowed to travel a three-day journey so that they may offer sacrifices and worship Jehovah God. Pharaoh responds, "Who is the Lord, that I should obey his voice to let Israel go? I know not the Lord, neither will I let Israel go."

But God was persistent to the tune of ten times asking Pharoah, and ten times sending plagues over the land.

For the same reason, because of the reticence and resistance of Pharoah, one must be persistent in winning a soul to salvation. One must be persistent in getting anyone out of captivity. One must be persistent in deliverance and insist on their own deliverance.

Ten speaks of the **main** *gods/goddesses* of Egypt because historians believe they worshipped hundreds and hundreds more. So, there was a *god* for everything in their culture.

Coming up against the Egyptian *god* of the Nile; the first Egyptian Plague was that the water was turned to blood.

Jesus' first miracle in the Gospels was to turn water into wine. Jacob had said in the Old Testament that Reuben was as unstable as water. Water can be turned into ice, into steam, or it can remain as water, it depends on the surrounding conditions. From the Bible, we learn that in judgment water can be turned into blood. And, from the Bible we learn that in celebration, water can be turned into wine.

Physiologically we are 70% water, *and* the Earth is 70% water—that tells me that we are malleable, moldable—changeable. If we are not sure of who we are and whose we are, we can be changed in form and turned into things that may not be the right things or Godly things.

In this first plague, all the fish died.

In the New Testament, Jesus told His fledgling Disciples, ***I will make you fishers of men.*** Folks, we are supposed to be doing the work of an evangelist and winning souls for the kingdom, being *fishers of men. If* we don't fulfill that duty, which, if we are created to do that, that is our worship, then unsaved men will die in their sin, and the Earth will **stink**.

When those who are called to be *sons* of God and given authority to become sons of God do not *become*, the Earth also suffers along with mankind.

Is the Earth currently suffering?

Yes, big time.

Saints of God, it is our fault, it is our problem, and we will have to answer for it for poor stewardship. Remember, we were put here to dress the Garden. The Garden is the Earth.

The second Egyptian deity that Jehovah dealt with was the *goddess* of fertility, water, and renewal, who had the head of a frog. *You want to* worship *frogs? Really?* Then God may have said, *Then, here you go.* You got frogs. Frogs were everywhere. Pharaoh double-downed on his stubbornness by getting his magicians to bring in more frogs, imitating the power of God.

Pharoah: God is not mocked.

Only Moses, by God, was able to make the frogs go away.

On the one hand we can see the Mercy of God because He could have just destroyed all the Egyptians in one fell swoop. But on the other hand, we can see that God is teaching both His people. He is saying, **Behold: I AM God.**

In addition, for those with eyes to see, God is showing how much He loves His own and what He will go through to rescue them. He is showing His diligence and teaching them faith and stick-to-it-ness. For those with teachable spirits, God is giving a master class with these plagues.

In His Mercy and willingness to redeem and draw mankind, God sent a judgment, a plague rather than turn the Egyptians over to death, but God's plan was to bring His people out of bondage and slavery so that they could come up and worship.

The next plague was lice from the dust of the earth. At the command of the Lord to Moses, Aaron was told to stretch forth his rod and smite the dust of the earth. When he did, the dust became lice, and it affected everybody.

The magicians of Pharaoh were humiliated, and had to tap out, professing, "This is the finger of God." They finally admitted that the God of Israel was greater than the *gods* they worshipped. The Greatest God, actually.

Still Pharoah did not relent.

**Next, God showed Himself mighty against** the Egyptian *god* of creation, movement of the Sun, rebirth; it had the head of a fly. Seriously, it seems the Egyptians will worship nearly anything and everything. ***The head of a fly.***

God will allow or send pestilence against your enemies, even swarms of flies against those who inhibit or completely stop your praise and your worship.

All this shows how God deals with folks according to their own hearts. God had dealt with the Hebrews according to their own hearts. The Hebrews kept practicing idolatry, so they got sent into captivity with the Egyptians. Seems to me, at that time that was either the capitol of idols, idolatry and false *gods* or the closest place to send the Hebrews that were being punished by getting an overdose of idolatry since they wouldn't stop it after many warnings.

God may have been saying something such as, **You want idolatry, here's some idolatry, and you will be there for 400 years as slaves.**

Egypt was afflicted with ten plagues, and while you may think that Israel got away scot-free, they didn't. They had a few plagues to deal with too. It wasn't until the fourth plague—flies—that God began to spare His people. Therefore, the Israelites had to deal with the water turning to blood, frogs, and gnats (lice).

The first three plagues were judgment against the *gods* of Egypt that Israel also needed to learn. God proved those *gods* powerless

God was separating His people from the Egyptians, and therefore, He needed to rid them of any idolatry they had assumed while living in Egypt.

Here comes the fourth plague: flies.

Again, Pharaoh hardened his heart or as the Word says God hardened Pharoah's heart. Whomever did it, Ramses II disregarded the request, resulting in the swarms of flies invading the land. This time, however, only the Egyptians are affected by this plague; the Hebrew slaves remain untouched.

What Pharoah and many of us don't realize is that the idol *gods, goddesses,* devils, demons, and whatever other evil spiritual entities we "worship" would run completely roughshod over us in no time flat if GOD wasn't restraining them. The Egyptian plagues prove this. For the plagues we usually think that God sent the evil. Saints of God think of it more like God pulled back His hand and those idols took it to the max against the Egyptians and anyone else who had invited them up from hell and empowered them to do their evil in the Earth.

Pharoah should have learned that when God speaks, when God says something, even those idols must obey; the must stand down, fall back and relent in their torment of and attacks on mankind.

If we'd ever be conscious of this then no one anywhere, at any time would ever call on a demon, devil, or idol *god* or *goddess*.

**Men ought not to be so foolish. When man calls on the devil or occultic powers with the belief or hope that they will get what they want from the devil or one of his demons, or idol *gods* they are seriously overplaying their hand.** Our mouths are to worship God, not to call on demonic entities. Our minds are to serve the Lord, not devise wickedness.

## There Is No Holy Cow

The Egyptian *goddess* of love and protection has the head of a cow. Protection--, from a cow? Wow!

The corresponding plague was the death of cattle and livestock. Pharoah was warned in advance that all the livestock would die if he didn't let God's people go and worship. But he did not let them go, so disease and pestilence fell upon the Egyptians' cattle, and those animals died.

Worshipping the sacrifice is like using worms to fish, while fish is the desired goal of the outing, you start worshipping the worm. People, please.

> For all the gods of the nations are idols: but the Lord made the heavens. (Psalm 96:5)

## Five More Plagues

Isis is the Egyptian *goddess* of medicine and peace. Saints, when we say a certain entity is the *god* or *goddess* of something that means to those people that they must worship that entity so bad things don't happen to them. As well, to them it means to worship them so the opposite of bad things will happen to them. It's convoluted, but they seem to know that if they don't worship all these things that what these entities represent will overtake them and make life tumultuous, troublesome, or impossible.

God doesn't work like that. He has plans of peace and a good outcome for us, but the Egyptians don't seem to know that. Also, has anyone else considered that in 400 years a million or more Hebrews didn't seem to proselytize much or any of Egypt? Even today, their main religion is Islam.

Have we not learned from life and foremost from the Word of God that worshipping something that you shouldn't worship will get you captured, either physically, spiritually, or both?

## Unclean

Back to the plagues.

The sixth plague was ashes turning to boils and sores on the Egyptians. Instructed by the Lord, Moses took ashes and threw it into the air. As the dust from the ashes blew all over Egypt, it settled on man and beast and formed boils and sores. God protected His people from this plague.

Egyptians were all about cleanliness, yet this $6^{th}$ plague pronounces the people "unclean." You worship an unclean thing, you become unclean. The magicians who have been seen throughout the previous plagues are unable to perform ceremonial rituals to their Egyptian *gods* and *goddesses* in this unclean state, are seen in this account no more.

Moses and Aaron are the only ones left standing in front of Pharaoh, since the unclean could no longer come before Pharoah.

Of note, saints of God, notice how many of these elements and animals witches use in their devilments, spells, and curses, even today. This gives us an idea as to what demons and idols witches are calling on to ask that evil things happen to the people of God. So, shouldn't we ask if these idols are worshipped by man, then why do they also turn on man and curse him?

Answered earlier, it is because they don't love mankind, they just want the worship. They are transactional and want what they want. These idols are invited and fed by humans who are also transactional and want what they want, devil may care, or scorch the Earth. Whether these people are like that initially or take on the nature of these evil idol *gods*, only the Lord knows. However, these idols' ultimate plan would be to turn on man and destroy him except for God restraining them.

By the Word and the decree of the Lord, the ocean can only go so far. Both the sun and the moon know their circuits. The stars stay suspended in the sky, else any and all of this could destroy this planet and mankind in an instant.

Worth repeating: Except the Lord by His Mercy, and our prayers restrain the evil that has already been let loose, they would run amok. For this reason, none of us should be prayerless. We should make the opportunity to pray to make declarations, decrees, and most importantly to agree with God. This is also part of why we were created and placed on Earth. This is how we steward spiritually; this is part of our worship. We worship by walking in the Spirit, praying by the Spirit, praying in the Truth and praying the Truth, which is the Word of God.

# Hail Fire

The Egyptian *goddess* of the sky is next confronted by the Lord. Next thing you know, hail was slamming down from the sky in the form of fire. It turned to fire as it hit the ground. Pharoah's magicians, if they were even clean enough to enter into his presence again, couldn't do that.

Only God.

Crops were destroyed. When the nation's food is affected, the Egyptians now must be concerned about matters of life or death--, after all, a man's gotta eat.

> And the flax and the barley was smitten: for the barley *was* in the ear, and the flax *was* bolled. But the wheat and the rie were not smitten: for they *were* not grown up. (Exodus 9:31-32)

Saints, what God won't do to come to you when you call. What God won't do to free you to come up and worship. As long as you are coming to worship sincerely, in Spirit and in Truth He will not only meet you there, as He inhabits the praises of His people. But if you are not free, if you are still captive and you desire, truly desire to worship the Lord, He will come or send a deliverer to break you out of bondage.

Again, Moses and Aaron approached Pharaoh with the same request, **"Let my people go so that they may serve me,"** and then they pronounced the judgment of locusts if not heeded.

**Because of worship to the** Egyptian *god* of storms and disorder, Seth, the next plague was locusts falling from the sky.

The eighth plague issued by the Lord showed the **strong hand of God** over all the other Egyptian *gods* and *goddesses*.

# The Light, the Glory

Ra is the Egyptian *god* of the sun. The complete dimming down of that *god's* perceived power was seen in the next plague; it was three days of complete darkness. Three days of thick, palpable darkness. The sun, the most worshipped *god* in Egypt other than Pharaoh himself, was shut down. After all, God made it. The thing you make can never be greater than the one who Created it. Turned off by God, the sun gave no light for three days. The Lord showed that He had control over the sun as a witness that the God of Israel had ultimate power over life and death.

This is echoed in the three hours of darkness when Jesus gave up the Ghost on the Cross. God again showed that He had complete authority and power over life and Death. Light is Life and darkness represents death.

Jesus had said and now He proved:

> No man taketh it from me, but I lay it down of myself. I have power to lay it down, and I have power to take it again. This commandment have I received of my Father. (John 10:18)

**Darkness, the complete absence of light was a representation of Death,** and is one of the *Family of Death*. One may suppose that the darkness that pervaded the land was thick with evil and demons. Devils and spiritual wickedness love darkness, it is their playground.

Still, Pharoah didn't give in.

After the Darkness was lifted, Pharaoh offered Moses another deal. Since virtually all of the Egyptian animals had been consumed by the judgments of the Lord, Pharaoh now consented to the request made, to let the people go, but they must leave their animals behind.

As far as Jehovah is concerned and as He made this known through Moses, this was a totally unacceptable offer, as the animals were to be used as the actual sacrifice to the Lord.

All of Creation was made to praise the Lord.

# What If You've Lost Your Sacrifice?

Can you, *Dear Reader*, take a moment to consider how much of a sacrifice **this** sacrifice would be? If all the Egyptian's cattle and livestock was wiped out, but the Hebrews had theirs and they were to be used in sacrifice, this was a **real** oblation to God.

When a sacrifice isn't felt, really felt by the giver is it really a sacrifice?

So, Jehovah God is telling 600K plus men, and if you count a certain way, some historians say as many as 3,000,000 Hebrews came out of Egypt to come up to worship, and bring their beasts for sacrifice. If there are 600K men and they are heads of households, then at least

600K head of cattle or other livestock would be sacrificed unto the Lord, while the folks back in Egypt had no cattle. They had no cattle because Pharoah wouldn't capitulate when God asked him to Let the People Come Up to Worship in the 5$^{th}$ plague, so all the cattle died.

Where's the beef? It will soon be on the way up to worship the Lord, the One True God. Egyptians, your plight is because of your dear leader, the one you worship, your Pharoah, Ramses II.

Of course, this demi-god is selfish and self-serving, wonder what he'll do for you, I mean *to* you next?

## Pharoah Spoke It

The Lord is uncompromising when He has set terms; He's God, and He's got it like that. As far as God is concerned, the people are coming out of bondage, whether Pharoah likes it or not, whether Pharoah agrees with it or not; whether Pharoah resists, lives, or dies – they are coming out.

The arrogance of Pharoah is astounding because they play for keeps, they play to the death. In his obstinance, Pharoah, himself pronounced the last deadly plague to be unleashed upon the land from his very own lips as he speaks to Moses.

> Get thee from me, take heed to thyself, see my face no more; for in that day thou seest my face thou shalt die.

And Moses said,

"Thus saith the Lord, About midnight will I go out into the midst of Egypt: And all the firstborn in the land of Egypt shall die, from the firstborn of Pharaoh that sitteth upon his throne, even unto the firstborn of the maidservant that is behind the mill; and all the firstborn of beasts. And there shall be a great cry throughout all the land of Egypt, such as there was none like it, nor shall be like it any more."

The tenth plague was extremely personal to Ramses II. Pharaoh who was worshipped as a *god* was now personally challenged. The firstborn is the beginning of every man's strength. The death of the firstborn can only be described as death itself. It is a horror, a nightmare to the parent. God took away the beginning of even Pharoah's strength.

**This plague did not touch the Hebrews, because of the Blood of the Passover Lamb.**

Pharoah spoke what the curse would be and since God was delivering His people; Period. God would no longer allowed Pharoah to curse them, or continue to curse them. **That curse immediately went BACK TO SENDER.** And to prove to them and all of Egypt, and even the whole world, that there is redemption for mankind, and redemption for his seed, and his strength, and his generations.

Saints of God, even if you are in captivity yourself right now, in Christ there is hope and hope of freedom for your generations.

> O give thanks unto the Lord; for he is good: for his mercy endureth for ever.
>
> (1) To him who alone doeth great wonders: for his mercy endureth for ever.
>
> (4) To him that smote Egypt in their firstborn: for his mercy endureth for ever: (Psalm 136:1,4)
>
> Give thanks to him who killed the firstborn of Egypt. His faithful love endures forever.(Psalm 136:10 NIV)

What was so unusual about Paul and Silas worshipping God while they were in jail was that those who are incarcerated don't have free will. And if they do, they usually don't worship, they usually complain and moan and murmur. But, especially notice that when Paul and Silas were busted out of jail, the jailer and his whole family got saved. That could have been the outcome for Pharoah and all of Egypt, but Pharoah took a different route, most likely influenced by any and all of the *gods* and *goddesses* and demons posing as deities in his head--, in his very soul.

Most likely those demons said to Pharoah: *Do not let them go. Chase them. Do not let them go. Kill them if you have to, but do not let them go*. These may have been the words of those influencing-demons, devils, and idols in the soul of Pharoah who also thought himself a god. Saints, a man thinks himself a *god*, when a false *god* has fully embedded itself into that man and taken over his soul. When that false *god*, which is a demon has taken over that man's mind, body, and life, the man will think that he is that entity. He will think that he is the *god* and he will fully take on the nature of that demon and behave as that demon. Pharoah was no *god*, but who could deliver a man who doesn't want to be delivered?

Repent of worshipping false *gods*. If you didn't realize that you were, I pray this book has opened your eyes. My book, **Lord, Let the Devil Overplay His Hand** has a chapter entitled, *Repent of False Worship* which has very good resources listed to find out how to repent of worshipping false deities, how to find lists of them, and how to divorce them forever.

## Before He Came Up to Worship- David

Where was David before he came to famously worship God? He was in a battle. He was in warfare. That is where any of us are because coming up to worship is first a decision and it is also a battle, every day and every time. But God will reprove kings for our sakes, saying:

*Touch not mine anointed, do my prophet no harm.* God wasn't having it.

**God came and got him and then he worshipped, or did God come and get him TO worship???** I challenge anyone that God will call you individually or collectively to worship and if you are not in a place to worship, God will bring you out of where you are so you not only can, but you will worship.

When the devil sees a strong anointing on a person, he is drawn to it and will use whomever he can to interfere with it, block it, or even try to remove it, usually through jealousy. Through prayer and worship anointing is made powerful and more powerful. The man who is anointed of God who continues to worship grows mightily in the Lord. The devil hates that, so David was a target as soon as Samuel anointed him king, even though he didn't ascend to the throne until many years later.

# Before They Came Up to Worship

Before He came back up to the Right Hand of God, Jesus was in Hell, pure and real Hell.

Before he came back into worship, Job was in a *hellified* situation.

Before they came back into worship Paul & Silas were in jail.

Before he came to worship, Paul was shipwrecked-- , more than once.

Before he came to worship, Apostle John was in exile in Patmos. For John it was more like he never stopped worshipping, even when he was in exile at Patmos. The goal is to never stop your worship. Yet in our day the devil has too often been successful in changing our location, the works of our hands, and the words that come out of our mouths. All those things affect outcomes, they affect our worship. They affect both the direction and the quality of our worship.

Before they came up to worship, the Hebrews were in slavery and heavily oppressed by the Egyptians. They were in a battle, and against Pharoah, that is a battle for their lives. But God called them up to worship. That might as well be a call for deliverance and freedom because when God calls you up to worship, you will heed that call, and you will go up to worship.

The man who sins but who won't repent will hide from God. God is the only one who can help him, so why is he hiding? God is the ONLY one who loves him, so why is He hiding? God created a whole Earth for him, feeds him, keeps him, protects him, provides for him, ---, so why is he hiding from God?

Then there is the person who takes all that God has provided away--, why be so foolish or ignorant or rebellious to run to that entity, the devil? When a man has been so deceived to run to his oppressor, he has really been deceived. Have you ever met or known someone that when you go to them with a problem and you tell them all about it, you know or find out later that while you were opening up to them, telling them of your hurt, loss, or need all they were doing was thinking of how what you were going through would benefit them? The devil is like that. The devil, a devil, devilish people are not the ones to run to, in trouble, or ever--, they are the ones to run *from*. And their "father" the devil the father of lies, deceit, trickery and all other things evil is the one to run from, not toward.

# Before *She* Came Up to Worship

Before she came up to worship Hannah was in a battle. Her battle was the usual, with Peninnah.

Deborah: A prophetess and judge worshipped—she and Barak sang a song of praise to the Lord after He used them to deliver Israel from the Canaanites. Before worship, Deborah was in battle.

Mary: The mother of God, who trusted in God despite ridicule and scorn. Except for God, even her own betrothed would have put her away. Yet she believed God. Faith is accounted for righteousness and faith is also worship.

Elizabeth was in a battle in her home. First, she was up in age before she ever conceived. In those days and even now you can only imagine what their conversations and arguments must have been like.

Once she conceived, God had to shut the mouth of her husband because he wanted to name the child that would be John the Baptist some wrong name—probably, *Jr.* A spouse being made mute is different than getting the silent treatment, but some of us know that evil punishment from a spouse is a battle. My ex could go as long as 2 weeks without speaking to me.

*What did I do in the meanwhile?*

Continue to worship the Lord, and as long as he was quiet, I'd work on writing a book--, the thing I was put on this Earth to do.

Martha worshipped the Lord after her brother was raised from the dead. That was an emotional and spiritual turmoil.

Abigail was the wife of Naboth. Her battle was also in the home--, a crazy husband who wouldn't honor David who had asked for a few provisions for his men and who had respected Naboth by watching over and not stealing his sheep.

Esther's battle was a national battle. Haman wanted to exterminate all the Jews. Esther called a three-day dry fast that moved the Hand of God in the favor of the Jews and also against Haman.

When the righteous are in authority, the people rejoice: but when the wicked beareth rule, the people mourn.(Proverbs 29:2)

The woman with the issue of blood had an internal spiritual battle, that surely affected her home and marriage--, if she had a natural husband. Yet when she reached Jesus and touched the hem of His garment, and her issued dried up, surely she worshipped the Lord. To know that Jesus is Lord, and believe it is also worship. One can worship and still be embattled. But it is because of the worship that we come through victoriously.

Mary Magdalene had to be delivered of seven devils. That is a battle. Was it oppression or full possession, the Word does not say, but Jesus personally delivered Mary Magdalene and then she worshipped, probably in the moment, but also continually by doing what she was called to do in this Earth. Mary Magdalene was a follower, Disciple, and Apostle of Jesus Christ.

If you are coming up to worship, the Lord will deliver you.

God knows your heart. If it will be business as usual after you get what you want from the Lord, then He won't race to your situation. If you are well seasoned and all in Christ, you will worship BEFORE the battle, before the war and even before the victory, but certainly afterwards. God deserves His praise and His worship. In Heaven they worship 24/7. How much worship have you given the Lord today?

## Moving Heaven & Earth

God will move Heaven and Earth to get to you. Wherever you are, lost, confused, captive – it doesn't matter. He heard the cries of the Hebrews enslaved in Egypt and He did just that--, He moved Heaven and Earth to get to them and to get them out of captivity.

God will hear your cries too.

He hears the cries of the Righteous.
(Psalm 34:17)

Lord, don't leave my soul in hell. When you deem, or finally recognize that where you are is **hell**… and cry to the Lord, and you are one of His, He will move Heaven and Earth to get you free.

You want deliverance?

Have you asked the Lord?

Have you indeed cried out? If your heart is pure and you intend to come up to worship and to worship in Spirit and in Truth, He will come for you. No matter what it takes, even ten plagues on your captor, on your enemy, even death to your spiritual opponent. We don't war against flesh and blood, but against spiritual wickedness.

Do you really think that God will send ten plagues on a Pharoah-captor--, and we don't even know how long that took. But do you think that God would invest that kind of time, effort, and power to get you set free from slavery and captivity and spiritual bondage, for you to just give Him a wave and say, *Thank you, man?* Do you think He'd do that for you to be free and just go on your way?

Nope. That's transactional. Do you think God would set you free, especially with the purpose of you coming up to worship, for you to not worship, but go back to living the same way that got you caught up in the first place?

When God says Let Them Come Up & Worship that is not only a command to Pharoah, it is a **mandate** to the slaves who will be set free and delivered to worship the Lord.

Worshipping in Spirit and Truth takes time; it is not one and done, and it is permanent, not temporary. It's not that you owe God for saving you, since salvation is a free gift, to us, but it cost Jesus everything. But you do owe appreciation, thanksgiving, praise, worship-- relationship. He is due worship and praise and honor and adoration. If the elders and those around the Throne of God are shouting, *Holy, Holy, Holy*, 24/7 then what He does is priceless. And, you don't worship because you are told to or because you are made to; you worship because you want to, because you are moved to. That is where the Truth comes in. You worship God in Spirit and in Truth.

## Told You So

I so dislike the told you so kind of friends and relatives. You can't unscramble eggs, so if you have made a mistake or more than one mistake having someone tell you, *I told you not to do that doesn't do anything for you.* It is a phrase that glorifies the one that "told you" as if they are a sage or a prophet or something. It strokes their ego and stokes their pride. Those are flesh words; if you are using them when you talk to people, stop it. It will only make them feel worse.

I'm not saying, *I told you so,* because I don't know you, but had you been worshipping God in Spirit and in Truth, the enemy would have left you alone. He would have gone right by you; you would have been too hot, too bright, too glorified for him to touch you. Were you hot or cold is what the Lord says – God wants you HOT.

- Lord, let me be too hot for the enemy that he passes me by because of the pain of trying to touch a burning one. Let him go blind for looking on the glory that you bestow on me for glorifying You. In the Name of Jesus, Amen.

Repent for not worshipping the Lord, as that is what we were made for. That is why we were put here.

Not worshipping the Lord is exactly how Lucifer fell idle and evil; Lucifer wasn't created evil. But his pride and jealousy of God is what caused that war to break out in Heaven. NOT worshipping the Lord God is how Lucifer fell from Heaven like lightning. Not worshipping God makes you more susceptible to sin, capture, and captivity and further distancing from worshipping God. No one wants a *You can't get there from here* situation in life, but that is always the devil's goal.

Serving idols means that you are serving those that hate God, are enemies of God, refuse to worship and honor the Lord, and are prideful and jealous of God. What you serve, what you worship, you take on the nature of. If you serve demons like that, eventually you will take on their nature. Just as I said earlier that when you worship God, He glorifies you. God's glorification of you means that you start to look like Him because He is glorious. He is altogether lovely, He is pure, He is honest, He is love. Eventually you take on the nature of Christ and you also start to be those things.

But when you serve idols, you start to look and smell like them. Stinky.

You want to be delivered? Follow the pattern of the Hebrews captive in Egypt for 430 years. Be saved, be *in Christ*. Proclaim and prophesy an end to your captivity. Now, **tell the Lord you**

**want to come up and worship.** Tell Him you want to come up to the high places and tear down the work of the enemy. Renounce idolatry and *whoredoms*. Repent and renounce ever having served any idols.

Tell Him that you want to **worship** Him in Spirit and Truth, committing or re-committing to proper and godly service and He will come and get you. Even if it takes ten plagues against your captor, even if you have TEN captors, even if you have the fullness of captors, the Lord will come and get you.

Even if it means death to your captor and having to completely destroy him, the LORD will rescue you from hell, from captivity, from slavery, from the land of idols. Look what happened to Pharoah; look how God contended with Ramses II for the sake of not only His people, but for the sake of His worship.

This is how merciful our Father is: even if you are the cause of yourself being there, even if your ancestors are the cause, even if your people have been there for 430 years, He will hear your cry and He will come and get you out, as long as you bring your sacrifice and come up to worship.

## Dear Reader

Thank you for acquiring, reading, and sharing this book. May the Lord show you if you are a victim or participant in idolatry and may He deliver you and strengthen you to resist all temptation.

May the Lord set you free to Come Up & Worship.

In the Name of Jesus,

**Amen.**

Dr. Marlene Miles

## Prayer books by this author

While most books by this author have prayer points either throughout the book or at the end, there are some books that are **only** prayers. You just open up the book and pray. They are listed below:

**Prayers Against Barrenness:** *For Success in Business and Life*

**Fruit of the Womb:** *Prayers Against Barrenness*

**Beauty Curses,** *Warfare Prayers Against*
https://a.co/d/5Xlc2OM

Courts of Marriage: Prayers for Marriage in the Courts of Heaven *(prayerbook)* https://a.co/d/cNAdgAq

Courtroom Warfare @ Midnight *(prayerbook)* https://a.co/d/5fc7Qdp

Demonic Cobwebs *(prayerbook)* https://a.co/d/fp9Oa2H

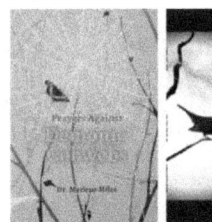

Every Evil Bird https://a.co/d/hF1kh1O

Every Evil Arrow https://a.co/d/afgRkiA

Gates of Thanksgiving

## Spirits of Death & the Grave, Pass Over Me and My House
https://a.co/d/dS4ewyr

*Please note that my name is spelled incorrectly on amazon, but not on the book.*

## Throne of Grace: Courtroom Prayer

https://a.co/d/fNMxcM9

## Warfare Prayer Against Poverty
https://a.co/d/bZ61lYu

Other books by this author

AK: *The Adventures of the Agape Kid*

AMONG SOME THIEVES

Ancestral Powers https://a.co/d/9prTyFf

Backstabbers https://a.co/d/gi8iBxf

Barrenness, *Prayers Against* https://a.co/d/feUltIs

Battlefield of Marriage, *The*

Blindsided: *Has the Old Man Bewitched You?* https://a.co/d/5O2fLLR

Break Free from Collective Captivity

Casting Down Imaginations https://a.co/d/1UxlLqa

Churchcraft: Witchcraft In the Church

Churchzilla, The Wanna-Be, Supposed-to-be Bride of Christ

Curses of Blind Men

Demonic Cobwebs (prayerbook)

Demonic Time Bombs

Demons Hate Questions

Devil Loves Trauma, *The*

Devil Weapons: Unforgiveness, Bitterness,...

The Devourers: *Thieves of Darkness 2*

Do Not Swear by the Moon

Don't Refuse Me, Lord (4 book series)
https://a.co/d/idP34LG

Dream Defilement

The Emptiers: *Thieves of Darkness, 1*
https://a.co/d/5I4n5mc

Every Evil Arrow
https://a.co/d/afgRkiA

Evil Touch https://a.co/d/gSGGpS1

Failed Assignment
https://a.co/d/3CXtjZY

Fantasy Spirit Spouse
https://a.co/d/hW7oYbX

FAT Demons (The): *Breaking Demonic Curses*

The Fold (5-book series)

- The Fold (Book 1)
- Name Your Seed (Book 2)
- The Poor Attitudes of Money (3)
- Do Not Orphan Your Seed (4)
- For the Sake of the Gospel (5)
- My Sowing Journal

Gang Ups: *Touch Not God's Anointed*

got HEALING? Verses for Life

got LOVE? Verses for Life

got HOPE? Verses for Life

got money? https://a.co/d/g2av41N

How to Dental Assist

How to Dental Assist2: Be Productive, Not Wasteful

I Take It Back

It's Coming Back: *Vengeance Is the Lord's, So Stop Making Weapons*

Legacy

Let Me Have A Dollar's Worth
https://a.co/d/h8F8XgE

Let Them Come Up & Worship

Level the Playing Field

Living for the NOW of God

Lose My Location
https://a.co/d/crD6mV9

Man Safari, *The*

Marriage Ed. Rules of Engagement & Marriage

Made Perfect in Love

Money Hunters: Beware of Those

Money on the Altar https://a.co/d/4EqJ2Nr

Mulberry Tree https://a.co/d/9nR9rRb

Motherboard (The) - *Soul Prosperity Series*

Name Your Seed

Occupy: *Until I Return*

Plantation Souls

Players Gonna Play

Power Money: Nine Times the Tithe
https://a.co/d/gRt41gy

The Power of Wealth *(forthcoming)*

Powers Above

Remember the Time https://a.co/d/3PbBjkF

Repent of Visiting Evil Altars
https://a.co/d/3n3Zjwx

The Robe, *Part 1, The Lessons of Joseph*

The Robe, *The Lessons of Joseph* Part II,

Seasons of Grief

Seasons of Waiting

Seasons of War

Second Marriage, Third--, *Any Marriage*

https://a.co/d/6m6GN4N

Seducing Spirits: *Idolatry & Whoredoms*

Sift You Like Wheat

Six Men Short: What Has Happened to all the Men?

Soul Prosperity, Soul Prosperity Series Book 3 https://a.co/d/5p8YvCN

Soulish & Diabolical Prayer Treatment

Souls In Captivity, Soul Prosperity Series Book 2

The Spirit of Poverty

StarStruck

SUNBLOCK

The Swallowers: *Thieves of Darkness*, Book 3

Take It Back

This Is NOT That: How to Keep Demons from Coming at You

Time Is of the Essence

Too Many Wives: *Why You Have Lady Problems*

Tormenting Spirits  https://a.co/d/dAogEJf

Toxic Souls

Triangular Power *(series)*

- Powers Above
- SUNBLOCK
- Do Not Swear by the Moon
- STARSTRUCK

Uncontested Doom

Unguarded Hours, *The*

Unseen Life, *The* https://a.co/d/0drZ5Ll

Unstable As Water: *Thou Shalt Not Excel*

Upgrade: How to Get Out of Survival Mode

- Toxic Souls (Book 2 of series)
- Legacy (Book 3 of series)

The Wasters: *Thieves of Darkness*, Bk 2
https://a.co/d/bUvI9Jo

What Have You to Declare? What Do You Have With You from Where You've Been?

When I Was A Child, *I Prayed As a Child*

When the Devourer is Rebuked

https://a.co/d/1HVv8oq

**The Wilderness Romance** *(series)* This series is about conducting a Godly relationship and marriage with someone who is a Wilderness person. It is about how to recognize it and navigate through it. These books are about how not to get caught up in such.

- *The Social Wilderness*

- *The Sexual Wilderness*
- *The Spiritual Wilderness*

# Other Series

## The Fold (a series on Godly finances)
https://a.co/d/4hz3unj

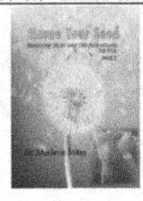

## Soul Prosperity Series https://a.co/d/bz2M42q

## Spirit Spouse books

https://a.co/d/9VehDSo

https://a.co/d/97sKOwm

## Thieves of Darkness series

**Triangular Powers** <https://a.co/d/aUCjAWC>

**Upgrade** (series) *How to Get Out of Survival Mode* https://a.co/d/aTERhX0